PRINCEWILL LAGANG

Biblical Dating: Finding Your Soul's Mate

First published by PRINCEWILL LAGANG 2023

Copyright © 2023 by Princewill Lagang

All rights reserved. No part of this publication may be reproduced, stored or transmitted in any form or by any means, electronic, mechanical, photocopying, recording, scanning, or otherwise without written permission from the publisher. It is illegal to copy this book, post it to a website, or distribute it by any other means without permission.

Princewill Lagang asserts the moral right to be identified as the author of this work.

First edition

This book was professionally typeset on Reedsy.
Find out more at reedsy.com

Contents

1	The Quest for Biblical Dating: Finding Your Soul's Mate	1
2	Preparing Your Heart for Love: The Foundations of Biblical...	4
3	Navigating the Journey: Meeting Potential Partners with...	7
4	Building a Strong Foundation: The Process of Getting to Know...	10
5	The Road to Commitment: Nurturing a Lasting Partnership	14
6	The Culmination of Love: Discernment and the Realization of...	17
7	Nurturing a Lifelong Love: Building a Strong and Lasting...	20
8	Thriving Together: Maintaining a Strong, Faith-Based...	23
9	Sharing Your Love Story with the World: Inspiring Others...	26
10	Reflecting on Your Journey: The Impact of Your Love Story	29
11	A Journey Without End: The Ever-Evolving Love Story	32
12	Embracing the Unknown: The Legacy of Faith-Based Love	35

1

The Quest for Biblical Dating: Finding Your Soul's Mate

In a world driven by fast-paced technology and fleeting connections, the search for a meaningful, enduring love story remains a fundamental human quest. This chapter, titled "The Quest for Biblical Dating: Finding Your Soul's Mate," will embark on a journey that explores the timeless wisdom of the Bible and how it can guide us towards a profound and lasting romantic partnership.

The Modern Dating Dilemma

As we dive into the world of biblical dating, we are confronted with the complexities of modern romance. The age of dating apps and swiping left or right has revolutionized the way we connect with potential partners. In the midst of this digital frenzy, many individuals find themselves longing for a more profound connection, a love story that transcends the superficiality of modern dating.

In this chapter, we will not dismiss the conveniences that technology brings to our lives but rather emphasize the importance of infusing our dating experiences with the age-old wisdom found within the pages of the Bible. The Bible, often perceived as an ancient text, contains invaluable guidance on the pursuit of love, partnership, and commitment that remains relevant today.

The Biblical Foundation

Before we embark on our journey through biblical dating, it is essential to establish the groundwork by understanding the core principles that underpin this approach. The Bible is not a rigid rulebook for dating but rather a collection of stories, parables, and teachings that provide timeless wisdom for building meaningful and lasting relationships.

1. Love, Grace, and Forgiveness: At the heart of biblical dating is the profound understanding of love as an act of grace and forgiveness. The Bible teaches us that love is patient, kind, and enduring, capable of overcoming past mistakes and transgressions. In embracing this concept, we learn to offer and accept forgiveness, nurturing relationships founded on genuine care and empathy.

2. Purpose and Commitment: Biblical dating encourages individuals to enter into relationships with a clear sense of purpose and commitment. It challenges us to consider the long-term potential of a relationship, encouraging us to seek partners who share our values, faith, and life goals.

3. Respect and Boundaries: The Bible also underscores the importance of mutual respect and setting boundaries in a relationship. These principles promote a healthy foundation for love, ensuring that both partners feel valued and safe in their emotional and physical interactions.

The Guiding Light

As we embark on our journey towards biblical dating, it is essential to acknowledge that this path is not without its challenges. It requires patience, introspection, and a deep understanding of the Bible's teachings. It invites us to explore our faith and spirituality, even if we have not previously done so.

In the chapters that follow, we will delve deeper into the practical aspects of biblical dating, addressing questions such as:

- How can we find potential partners who share our faith and values?
   - What does it mean to date with the intention of marriage?
   - How can we integrate biblical principles into our everyday dating experiences?

Through these explorations, we aim to provide you with the tools and insights necessary to embark on a journey towards a love that is rooted in biblical wisdom, a love story that may just lead you to your soul's mate.

2

Preparing Your Heart for Love: The Foundations of Biblical Dating

In the previous chapter, we embarked on a journey to discover the timeless wisdom of biblical dating. We laid the groundwork by exploring the core principles that underpin this approach. Now, in Chapter 2, "Preparing Your Heart for Love: The Foundations of Biblical Dating," we delve deeper into the foundational steps needed to embark on a journey of finding your soul's mate guided by biblical wisdom.

Self-Reflection and Faith

Before you can seek out your soul's mate, it's essential to begin with self-reflection and a strong foundation of faith. This chapter will guide you through the initial stages of your journey.

1. Self-Reflection: To find the right partner, you must first understand yourself. What are your values, beliefs, and life goals? Reflect on your past relationships and experiences to identify patterns, preferences, and areas of personal growth. Self-awareness is the cornerstone of biblical dating, allowing you to enter a relationship with a clear sense of self.

2. Strengthening Your Faith: A deep connection with your faith is crucial in biblical dating. This chapter will offer insights on how to strengthen your faith through prayer, study, and community involvement. A strong spiritual foundation will not only guide you but also help you attract like-minded individuals who share your faith and values.

Identifying Compatibility

Finding your soul's mate requires more than just faith and self-awareness. It necessitates identifying compatibility on various levels.

1. Spiritual Compatibility: The Bible emphasizes the importance of being "equally yoked" in your faith. This means finding a partner who shares your spiritual beliefs and values. This chapter will help you understand how to identify and nurture spiritual compatibility in a potential partner.

2. Emotional Compatibility: Emotional connection and intimacy are vital in a romantic relationship. Discover the biblical principles of empathy, kindness, and emotional connection. Learn how to create a safe and nurturing space for emotional sharing within a relationship.

3. Intellectual and Lifestyle Compatibility: Biblical dating is not just about faith; it's about sharing a life with someone who aligns with your values and goals. Explore how to identify compatibility in interests, lifestyles, and long-term aspirations.

Building Healthy Boundaries

Biblical dating promotes respect, honor, and the establishment of healthy boundaries. This chapter will guide you through this crucial aspect.

1. Physical Boundaries: The Bible encourages physical purity and modesty. Understand the importance of setting clear physical boundaries in your

relationship to honor both yourself and your partner.

2. Emotional Boundaries: Emotional boundaries are essential to maintain a healthy balance in your relationship. Learn how to communicate your feelings and needs effectively while respecting your partner's boundaries.

3. Time Boundaries: In our busy world, time is a precious resource. This chapter explores the importance of managing time wisely in your dating journey, allowing you to maintain other aspects of your life and faith.

Preparing for Marriage

While biblical dating is not solely focused on marriage, it encourages intention and commitment in relationships. This chapter will guide you on how to prepare for the possibility of marriage, emphasizing the importance of discernment, accountability, and long-term goals.

A Path to Authentic Love

As you progress through this chapter, you'll lay the foundation for a biblical dating journey filled with authenticity, faith, self-awareness, and compatibility. It's a path that leads you closer to finding your soul's mate, someone who shares your faith, values, and the desire to build a lasting and profound love story guided by the wisdom of the Bible.

3

Navigating the Journey: Meeting Potential Partners with Purpose

In Chapter 3 of "Biblical Dating: Finding Your Soul's Mate," we explore the practical aspects of navigating the dating journey with purpose and intention. This chapter is titled "Navigating the Journey: Meeting Potential Partners with Purpose."

Seeking with Intention

Biblical dating encourages us to approach the search for a soulmate with intention. In this chapter, we will delve into the steps necessary to meet potential partners thoughtfully.

1. Prayer and Guidance: We begin by emphasizing the significance of prayer in your dating journey. Seek guidance from a higher power, asking for wisdom in making choices and discerning the right path. Trusting in your faith and spirituality can help you make sound decisions.

2. Community and Accountability: The Bible highlights the importance of community and accountability in our lives. This chapter will discuss how building a supportive network of friends and mentors can offer guidance and

wisdom as you seek a soulmate.

3. Dating Platforms: Modern technology has expanded our dating options, but it's essential to use them wisely. This section offers guidance on utilizing dating platforms while maintaining the principles of biblical dating.

Identifying Potential Partners

Once you have set the stage for your dating journey, it's time to identify potential partners who align with your faith, values, and goals.

1. Shared Values: Discover how to assess a potential partner's values, beliefs, and character. Learn to ask the right questions to gauge compatibility and shared principles.

2. Red Flags: This section will guide you on recognizing red flags in potential partners, helping you avoid relationships that might not align with your faith and values.

3. The Role of Friends and Family: The input of your friends and family can be invaluable. This chapter discusses how to involve loved ones in your dating journey, benefitting from their wisdom and perspective.

Dating with Purpose

Biblical dating encourages dating with a sense of purpose and commitment. This chapter addresses the following aspects:

1. Intentional Dating: Explore how to approach dating as a meaningful step toward a lasting relationship. Learn how to set intentions, maintain your values, and communicate your goals with a potential partner.

2. Getting to Know Each Other: This section offers guidance on how to

build a deep connection while adhering to biblical principles. It encourages emotional intimacy and understanding between you and your potential partner.

3. Discernment: Biblical dating emphasizes the importance of discerning whether a relationship is God's will. Learn how to assess the compatibility, health, and long-term potential of your partnership.

Fostering Healthy Communication

Effective communication is a cornerstone of a successful relationship. This chapter explores how to communicate effectively with your potential partner, express your feelings and needs, and ensure both parties feel heard and respected.

Trusting the Process

This chapter concludes with a discussion on trusting the dating process, letting go of anxiety, and surrendering to God's plan. Embracing patience, faith, and self-awareness can lead you closer to finding your soul's mate guided by biblical wisdom.

As you navigate the dating journey with purpose, you open the doors to authentic, fulfilling relationships that are rooted in faith, self-awareness, and shared values. In the subsequent chapters of this book, we will delve even deeper into the nuances of biblical dating, ultimately guiding you toward discovering a love that resonates with the wisdom of the Bible.

4

Building a Strong Foundation: The Process of Getting to Know Your Potential Soulmate

In Chapter 4 of "Biblical Dating: Finding Your Soul's Mate," we embark on the next stage of the journey, focusing on the process of getting to know your potential soulmate. This chapter is titled "Building a Strong Foundation: The Process of Getting to Know Your Potential Soulmate."

Cultivating Emotional Intimacy

Emotional intimacy is a crucial component of any deep and meaningful relationship. In this chapter, we explore how to nurture this aspect of your connection with a potential partner:

1. Open and Honest Communication: We emphasize the importance of open, honest, and vulnerable communication. You'll learn how to express your thoughts, feelings, and desires while creating a safe space for your potential soulmate to do the same.

2. Active Listening: Building emotional intimacy involves active listening. We discuss how to truly hear and understand what your partner is saying, allowing you to strengthen your connection.

3. Shared Experiences: Sharing experiences and activities can deepen your emotional bond. This chapter provides guidance on how to create memorable moments and build a reservoir of shared memories.

Assessing Compatibility

As you continue to explore your connection with your potential soulmate, you'll need to assess compatibility. This section delves into the various aspects of compatibility:

1. Spiritual Compatibility: We revisit the concept of being "equally yoked" and explore how to ensure that you and your potential partner continue to align in your faith and values.

2. Lifestyle Compatibility: Lifestyle choices and long-term goals play a crucial role in a lasting relationship. Learn how to identify and navigate lifestyle differences while maintaining harmony in your partnership.

3. Conflict Resolution: Conflict is a natural part of any relationship. This chapter offers strategies for resolving conflicts in a healthy and constructive manner, ensuring that disagreements don't jeopardize the connection you're building.

Navigating Challenges

The path to finding your soulmate is not always smooth. This chapter acknowledges the potential challenges you may face and provides guidance on overcoming them:

1. External Pressures: Family, cultural expectations, and societal pressures can influence your relationship. Learn how to navigate these external factors while maintaining your commitment to your potential soulmate.

2. Timing and Patience: Timing is a crucial element in finding your soulmate. Understand the importance of patience and trusting in divine timing as you navigate the challenges of the dating journey.

Staying True to Biblical Principles

Throughout the process of getting to know your potential soulmate, it's essential to stay true to biblical principles. This chapter reinforces the importance of maintaining your faith and values in all aspects of your relationship.

The Role of Accountability

Accountability is a recurring theme in biblical dating. This chapter highlights the significance of involving mentors, friends, and trusted individuals in your relationship. Their guidance and support can provide valuable insights and help you maintain a healthy connection with your potential soulmate.

The Joy of Discovery

Getting to know your potential soulmate should be a joyous and fulfilling experience. This chapter concludes by reminding you to embrace the wonder of discovery and continue nurturing your emotional bond as you progress toward the possibility of a lasting and profound love story.

As you embark on the process of getting to know your potential soulmate, you deepen your connection, assess compatibility, and navigate challenges with the wisdom of biblical dating. In the upcoming chapters of this book, we'll delve further into the journey, examining the intricacies of commitment, discernment, and the potential path to a lifelong partnership.

5

The Road to Commitment: Nurturing a Lasting Partnership

In Chapter 5 of "Biblical Dating: Finding Your Soul's Mate," we shift our focus towards the road to commitment, where you'll learn how to nurture and strengthen the connection with your potential soulmate. This chapter is titled "The Road to Commitment: Nurturing a Lasting Partnership."

The Significance of Commitment

Biblical dating places a strong emphasis on commitment, and this chapter begins by exploring the profound significance of commitment in a relationship:

1. Defining Commitment: We delve into the various aspects of commitment, including emotional, spiritual, and physical commitment. Learn how commitment forms the backbone of a healthy, lasting partnership.

2. Commitment to God: Your commitment to each other is intertwined with your commitment to God. We discuss the importance of including God in the core of your relationship, continually seeking His guidance and blessings.

Deepening Spiritual Connection

As your relationship progresses, it is essential to continually deepen your spiritual connection:

1. Shared Spiritual Practices: Discover the beauty of engaging in shared spiritual practices, such as prayer, worship, and studying scripture together. These activities can help you and your potential soulmate grow closer spiritually.

2. Spiritual Accountability: Maintaining accountability in your faith journey is crucial. This chapter highlights the significance of keeping each other spiritually grounded and focused on your shared values.

Preparing for Marriage

While not every biblical dating relationship may lead to marriage, it is essential to prepare for this possibility. This section offers guidance on preparing for the sacrament of marriage:

1. Marriage as a Covenant: We explore the biblical concept of marriage as a covenant, emphasizing the importance of understanding the sacred nature of this commitment.

2. Marriage Preparation: This chapter outlines the steps involved in preparing for marriage, such as pre-marital counseling and seeking guidance from trusted mentors.

The Role of Family and Community

Your family and community play a vital role in your journey toward commitment. This chapter delves into the importance of involving them:

1. Family Support: Learn how to seek the support and blessings of your families, recognizing that their support can provide you with valuable insights and strengthen your commitment.

2. Community Blessing: Involving your church community and mentors can further enrich your journey toward commitment. Their blessings and guidance can provide you with a sense of unity and purpose.

Maintaining Healthy Boundaries

Healthy boundaries continue to be a crucial component of your relationship. This chapter discusses the importance of maintaining physical, emotional, and time boundaries as you journey toward commitment.

The Joy of Discernment

The path to commitment should be a joyful and enlightening one. This chapter concludes by emphasizing the importance of discernment, patience, and trust in the process. Enjoy the journey, savor the growth, and cherish the moments that bring you closer to finding your soul's mate.

As you nurture your relationship on the road to commitment, you deepen your spiritual connection, prepare for marriage, and involve your family and community in the journey. In the upcoming chapters, we'll explore the final steps of discernment and the potential realization of your dream to build a lasting and profound love story guided by the wisdom of the Bible.

6

The Culmination of Love: Discernment and the Realization of Your Soul's Mate

In Chapter 6 of "Biblical Dating: Finding Your Soul's Mate," we approach the culmination of your journey—a deep exploration of discernment and the realization of your soul's mate. This chapter is titled "The Culmination of Love: Discernment and the Realization of Your Soul's Mate."

The Art of Discernment

Discernment is a crucial aspect of biblical dating, guiding you toward making informed decisions about your relationship's future:

1. Defining Discernment: We start by clarifying what discernment means in the context of biblical dating. Discernment is the process of seeking divine guidance to make informed choices about your relationship's direction.

2. Prayer and Meditation: This chapter delves into the power of prayer and meditation as tools for discernment. You'll learn how to use these practices to gain insight and clarity about your relationship.

Seeking Divine Guidance

Divine guidance plays a pivotal role in discernment. This section focuses on seeking God's will for your relationship:

1. Trusting God's Plan: Discover the importance of trusting in God's plan for your love life. Even if your relationship takes an unexpected turn, remember that God's plan is always working for your ultimate good.

2. Recognizing Signs: We explore how to recognize signs and nudges from the divine in your relationship. These signs can offer valuable insights into your compatibility and the path forward.

Decision-Making

As you approach a point of decision-making, several key factors come into play:

1. Seeking Counsel: This chapter highlights the importance of seeking counsel from trusted mentors, friends, and spiritual leaders. Their wisdom and perspectives can be instrumental in your decision-making process.

2. Conversations with Your Partner: Engage in open and honest conversations with your potential soulmate about the future of your relationship. This chapter provides guidance on how to communicate your thoughts, feelings, and aspirations effectively.

Realizing Your Soul's Mate

The culmination of your journey is the realization of your soul's mate. This section celebrates the realization and offers guidance on what comes next:

1. Celebrating Your Love: Take time to celebrate the love you've discovered

on this journey. Recognize the deep connection, shared values, and spiritual alignment that have brought you to this point.

2. Preparation for Marriage: If marriage is the path you choose, this chapter discusses the importance of continued preparation for this sacred commitment. It also explores the process of proposing and planning for the wedding.

A Love Rooted in Faith

This chapter concludes with a reflection on the profound love you've cultivated, guided by the principles of biblical dating. Whether you've found your soul's mate or are continuing on your journey, your love story is deeply rooted in faith, self-awareness, shared values, and the wisdom of the Bible.

In the following chapters, we'll explore how to navigate the joys and challenges of a lifelong partnership built on the strong foundation of biblical dating. Whether you're embarking on this path or have already found your soul's mate, your journey is a testament to the power of faith and love.

7

Nurturing a Lifelong Love: Building a Strong and Lasting Marriage

In Chapter 7 of "Biblical Dating: Finding Your Soul's Mate," we shift our focus to the continuation of your journey, exploring the joys and challenges of building a strong and lasting marriage. This chapter is titled "Nurturing a Lifelong Love: Building a Strong and Lasting Marriage."

The Sacred Union of Marriage

Marriage is a sacred covenant, and this chapter begins by exploring the profound significance of this commitment:

1. Understanding Marriage as a Covenant: We revisit the biblical concept of marriage as a covenant, emphasizing the sacred nature of this union.

2. The Role of Faith: Your faith and spirituality continue to be pivotal in your marriage. We discuss the importance of keeping God at the center of your relationship, seeking His guidance and blessings as you journey together.

Cultivating a Christ-Centered Marriage

A Christ-centered marriage is characterized by love, grace, and faith. This section focuses on how to nurture such a marriage:

1. Prayer and Worship: Embrace the practice of prayer and worship as a couple. We delve into how these shared spiritual activities can deepen your connection and faith.

2. Spiritual Growth: Encourage each other's spiritual growth by engaging in the study of scripture and spiritual literature together. Strengthen your faith as a couple and individually.

Building Strong Foundations

Every strong and lasting marriage is built on solid foundations. This section offers guidance on nurturing the key components of your partnership:

1. Communication: Effective communication is essential in a marriage. Learn how to maintain open, honest, and empathetic dialogue, ensuring your connection remains strong.

2. Conflict Resolution: Disagreements are inevitable, but how you handle them matters. This chapter discusses strategies for resolving conflicts in a healthy and constructive manner, promoting understanding and growth.

3. Quality Time: Continue to invest in your relationship by spending quality time together. Find new ways to create lasting memories and keep the flame of love alive.

Family and Community

The role of family and community remains important in marriage. This section delves into the significance of involving them:

1. Family Blessings: Your families' support and blessings are invaluable. We discuss how to maintain a strong connection with your families and create a harmonious family network.

2. Community Support: Involving your church community and mentors can further enrich your marriage. Their blessings and guidance can provide a sense of unity and purpose.

Navigating Challenges

No marriage is without its challenges. This chapter acknowledges the potential hurdles you may face and provides guidance on overcoming them:

1. External Pressures: Family expectations, cultural differences, and societal pressures can influence your marriage. Learn how to navigate these external factors while maintaining your commitment to each other.

2. Maintaining Boundaries: Healthy boundaries continue to be a crucial aspect of your marriage. This section discusses the importance of maintaining physical, emotional, and time boundaries as you nurture your relationship.

The Joys of a Lifelong Partnership

This chapter concludes by celebrating the joys and fulfillment of a lifelong partnership built on the wisdom of biblical dating. Your journey, guided by faith, shared values, and a deep connection, is a testament to the power of love rooted in biblical principles.

In the following chapters, we'll continue to explore the intricacies of a lasting and profound love story, providing guidance on maintaining a strong, faith-based marriage and deepening your connection with your soul's mate.

8

Thriving Together: Maintaining a Strong, Faith-Based Marriage

In Chapter 8 of "Biblical Dating: Finding Your Soul's Mate," we continue to delve into the dynamics of a lasting and profound love story. This chapter is titled "Thriving Together: Maintaining a Strong, Faith-Based Marriage."

The Ongoing Journey

A faith-based marriage is not a destination but a journey. This chapter begins by emphasizing that your marriage continues to evolve and grow:

1. The Ever-Evolving Connection: Understand that your relationship is dynamic, with new challenges and opportunities emerging as you journey together. Continuously nurturing your connection is key to a thriving marriage.

Sustaining a Christ-Centered Marriage

As the foundation of your faith-based marriage, Christ remains at the center of your journey:

1. Daily Devotion: Embrace daily prayer, worship, and reflection as a couple. These practices keep Christ in the forefront of your lives and reinforce the spiritual bond between you.

2. Shared Ministry: Consider engaging in shared ministry or community service. Contributing to the greater good as a couple strengthens your faith and connection with each other.

Effective Communication

Effective communication remains an essential element in a thriving marriage:

1. Active Listening: Continue to actively listen and understand each other. Your evolving experiences and perspectives necessitate open, empathetic communication.

2. Healthy Conflict Resolution: As your relationship matures, conflicts may arise. Strengthen your skills in resolving disagreements constructively, ensuring your connection remains healthy and harmonious.

Building a Family Together

If you choose to have a family, this section offers guidance on the journey of parenthood:

1. Shared Values in Parenting: Define your shared values in parenting and create a harmonious approach to raising children within the context of your faith.

2. Family Support: Your extended family plays an important role in your family life. We discuss how to maintain positive relationships with your

families while prioritizing the well-being of your own family unit.

Strengthening Boundaries

Boundaries continue to be a cornerstone of a strong marriage:

1. Maintaining Emotional Intimacy: As your lives evolve, find new ways to nurture emotional intimacy and keep your connection deep and meaningful.

2. Time Management: Balancing your time between work, family, and personal growth is essential. This chapter provides guidance on effective time management to ensure your marriage remains a priority.

Navigating Midlife and Beyond

The challenges and joys of midlife and later years are unique. This section discusses how to navigate this phase of your journey:

1. Rediscovering Each Other: Explore ways to rediscover each other as you both change and grow through the years.

2. Legacy and Impact: Reflect on the legacy you wish to leave and how your faith and love story can impact the world around you.

The Journey Continues

This chapter concludes by recognizing that your faith-based marriage is an ongoing journey. By nurturing your faith, commitment, and love, you ensure that your love story continues to thrive and inspire others.

In the following chapters, we'll continue to explore the intricacies of a lasting, profound love story, providing guidance on deepening your connection, maintaining a strong marriage, and sharing your wisdom with the world.

9

Sharing Your Love Story with the World: Inspiring Others through Faith-Based Love

In Chapter 9 of "Biblical Dating: Finding Your Soul's Mate," we focus on the significance of sharing your love story with the world and inspiring others through your faith-based love. This chapter is titled "Sharing Your Love Story with the World: Inspiring Others through Faith-Based Love."

The Impact of Your Love Story

Your love story, rooted in faith and guided by biblical principles, has the potential to inspire and guide others on their own journey to finding love:

1. Sharing Your Testimony: Understand the power of sharing your testimony with others. By recounting your experiences and the role of faith in your love story, you can provide hope and encouragement to those seeking meaningful, lasting relationships.

2. Mentoring and Support: Consider offering mentorship and support to

individuals who are embarking on their own journeys of faith-based love. Your wisdom and experiences can be invaluable to those seeking guidance.

Strengthening Your Community

Your love story can contribute to the strength and unity of your faith community:

1. Community Engagement: Actively participate in your church and faith community. By sharing your love story and offering guidance, you can contribute to the faith-based relationships within your community.

2. Supporting Young Couples: Consider supporting and mentoring young couples within your community, helping them navigate the challenges and joys of faith-based love.

Leaving a Legacy

Your love story, deeply rooted in faith, is a legacy that can impact generations:

1. Legacy Building: Reflect on the legacy you wish to leave for your children, grandchildren, and future generations. Consider how your love story can serve as a model of faith-based love and commitment.

2. Faith-Focused Parenting: If you have children, explore ways to raise them within the context of your faith and love story. Share your experiences and values with them, passing down the wisdom you've gained.

Nurturing Your Connection

Throughout your journey of inspiring others, it's essential to continue nurturing your own connection:

1. Date Nights: Make time for regular date nights to maintain the spark and intimacy in your relationship.

2. Retreats and Getaways: Consider taking retreats or getaways to strengthen your bond and create new memories together.

Gratitude and Reflection

This chapter concludes with a call to express gratitude for the love and faith that has guided your journey. Reflect on your experiences, the challenges you've overcome, and the growth you've achieved.

Your love story is not just a personal journey; it's a testament to the power of faith-based love. By sharing your experiences and inspiring others, you contribute to a world where meaningful, lasting relationships are built on a foundation of faith and biblical principles.

In the final chapter of this book, we'll reflect on your entire journey and the impact you've made in the world through your love story.

10

Reflecting on Your Journey: The Impact of Your Love Story

In Chapter 10, the final chapter of "Biblical Dating: Finding Your Soul's Mate," we conclude your journey with a reflection on the impact of your love story. This chapter is titled "Reflecting on Your Journey: The Impact of Your Love Story."

A Journey of Faith

Your journey to find your soul's mate, guided by biblical principles and rooted in faith, has been a remarkable one. This chapter begins by emphasizing the significance of faith throughout your journey:

1. Celebrating Your Faith: Take a moment to celebrate the role of faith in your love story. Your unwavering belief in God's plan and guidance has been the driving force behind your successful journey.

2. Gratitude: Express gratitude for the opportunities, challenges, and growth you've experienced. Recognize the role of gratitude in maintaining a strong and loving relationship.

The Wisdom of Biblical Dating

This section revisits the core principles of biblical dating and highlights how they have enriched your love story:

1. Love, Grace, and Forgiveness: The foundation of your relationship has been love, grace, and forgiveness. Reflect on the role of these principles in nurturing a loving partnership.

2. Purpose and Commitment: Your journey has been characterized by purpose and commitment. Consider how these elements have allowed you to navigate challenges and build a strong, lasting relationship.

The Legacy of Your Love Story

Your love story, deeply rooted in faith, has the potential to inspire and impact the world. Reflect on the legacy you're leaving:

1. Inspiring Others: Acknowledge the people you've inspired along the way. Your love story has the power to provide hope, guidance, and encouragement to others seeking meaningful relationships.

2. Building Strong Communities: Consider the role you've played in strengthening your faith community by sharing your experiences and offering mentorship.

3. A Legacy of Faith: Reflect on the legacy of faith you're creating for your children, grandchildren, and future generations. Your love story serves as a model of faith-based love and commitment.

Nurturing Your Connection

As you conclude your journey, it's essential to continue nurturing your own connection:

1. Growth and Reflection: Reflect on the growth you've experienced as individuals and as a couple. Consider how your love story has evolved over time.

2. Planning for the Future: Discuss your aspirations for the future and the goals you wish to achieve as a couple. Continue setting intentions and working together to realize your dreams.

The Joy of Your Love Story

This final chapter concludes by emphasizing the joy, fulfillment, and strength of your love story:

1. Celebrating Love: Take time to celebrate the love you've discovered and nurtured through your faith-based journey. Recognize the deep connection, shared values, and spiritual alignment that have been the cornerstones of your relationship.

2. Continued Gratitude: Express ongoing gratitude for the love, faith, and wisdom that have guided your journey and brought you to this point.

Your love story is a testament to the power of faith-based love. As you conclude this book and continue on your journey, remember that your relationship is a source of inspiration and guidance for others, a legacy of faith, love, and commitment.

May your love story continue to flourish, impacting the world through the wisdom of biblical dating and the strength of your faith.

11

A Journey Without End: The Ever-Evolving Love Story

In Chapter 11 of "Biblical Dating: Finding Your Soul's Mate," we explore the concept that a love story guided by faith is a journey without end. This chapter is titled "A Journey Without End: The Ever-Evolving Love Story."

The Ongoing Story

Your love story, deeply rooted in faith, is an ever-evolving narrative:

1. The Beauty of Growth: Recognize the beauty in the growth and evolution of your love story. As you continue to learn, adapt, and nurture your connection, your love deepens.

2. Shared Goals: Continue to set shared goals, dream together, and work toward realizing your aspirations. Your journey together is a collaborative endeavor.

Celebrating Milestones

Throughout your journey, there are various milestones and moments to celebrate:

1. Anniversaries: Celebrate the anniversaries of your marriage and the significant moments of your journey. Reflect on how far you've come and the adventures that lie ahead.

2. Milestones with Children: If you have children, celebrate their milestones and achievements. As a family, acknowledge their growth and development.

Sharing Wisdom

Your love story, a testament to faith-based love, offers wisdom that can inspire others:

1. Mentoring and Support: Continue to offer mentorship and support to individuals who seek guidance in their own faith-based relationships. Your experiences can be invaluable.

2. Community Engagement: Remain actively engaged in your faith community, sharing your experiences and offering encouragement to others who are on a similar journey.

Faith as the North Star

The foundation of your journey is your faith. Continually return to your faith as your North Star:

1. Prayer and Reflection: Engage in regular prayer and reflection to ensure your connection with your faith remains strong.

2. Shared Spirituality: Continue to cultivate your shared spiritual practices and activities. Deepen your bond through worship, study, and spiritual

exploration.

Nurturing Your Connection

As you continue your love story, it's essential to nurture your connection:

1. Quality Time: Invest in regular quality time together. Explore new experiences and create lasting memories that strengthen your bond.

2. Maintaining Communication: Keep your lines of communication open and honest. Discuss your thoughts, feelings, and dreams as your journey unfolds.

The Joy of a Love Story Without End

This chapter concludes by celebrating the joy, fulfillment, and strength of a love story without end:

1. Continued Gratitude: Express gratitude for the love, faith, and wisdom that guide your ever-evolving journey.

2. The Legacy of a Lifetime: Recognize that your love story is a legacy that will impact not only your lives but the lives of those you inspire along the way.

Your love story is a testament to the power of faith-based love. As you continue to write the chapters of your ever-evolving narrative, may your journey be filled with love, faith, and a profound sense of purpose.

12

Embracing the Unknown: The Legacy of Faith-Based Love

In Chapter 12, the final chapter of "Biblical Dating: Finding Your Soul's Mate," we explore the legacy of faith-based love and the beauty of embracing the unknown. This chapter is titled "Embracing the Unknown: The Legacy of Faith-Based Love."

The Uncharted Future

Your love story, deeply rooted in faith and guided by biblical principles, has led you to this point. The future is filled with endless possibilities:

1. A Journey of Faith: Acknowledge the journey of faith that has brought you to this moment. Embrace the unknown with the same unwavering belief in God's plan that has guided your love story.

2. Continued Growth: Understand that your journey is an ongoing process of growth and discovery. The future holds opportunities for you to learn, adapt, and nurture your love story further.

Celebrating Your Love Story

Throughout your journey, there are numerous moments to celebrate:

1. Anniversaries: Continue celebrating the anniversaries of your marriage and the significant moments in your journey. Reflect on the joy, love, and growth you've experienced.

2. Milestones with Children: If you have children, cherish their milestones and achievements. As a family, honor their accomplishments and the love that binds you together.

Inspiring Others

Your love story, a testament to faith-based love, has the power to inspire and guide others:

1. Mentorship and Support: Maintain your commitment to offering mentorship and support to individuals embarking on their own journeys of faith-based love. Your experiences and wisdom can be invaluable to those seeking guidance.

2. Community Engagement: Continue actively engaging with your faith community, sharing your love story, and providing encouragement to others on a similar path.

A Legacy of Faith

As you reflect on the legacy you're creating, consider the impact of your faith-based love:

1. Modeling Faith: Your love story serves as a model of faith, love, and commitment. Understand the influence your relationship can have on future

generations and the world around you.

2. Raising Faithful Children: If you have children, instill faith in their lives and share your love story as a testament to the power of faith-based love. Your values and experiences can shape their own journeys.

The Ongoing Journey

This chapter concludes by emphasizing that your journey is ongoing:

1. The Joy of Discovery: Embrace the joy of continually discovering each other. Your love story is an evolving narrative filled with opportunities for connection and growth.

2. Gratitude: Express ongoing gratitude for the love, faith, and wisdom that guide your ever-evolving journey. Recognize the profound impact your love story has on your lives and the lives of those you inspire.

Your love story, deeply rooted in faith and guided by biblical principles, is a legacy of love, grace, and commitment. As you continue your journey, may you embrace the unknown with the same unwavering faith that has brought you this far.

May your love story continue to inspire others, shaping the world with the power of faith-based love and the beauty of embracing the unknown.

Book Summary: "Biblical Dating: Finding Your Soul's Mate"

"Biblical Dating: Finding Your Soul's Mate" is an insightful and comprehensive guide to navigating the world of dating and relationships while staying true to your faith and biblical principles. This book takes readers on a journey through the stages of faith-based love, from the initial spark of attraction to the ongoing, ever-evolving love story.

Chapter 1: The Foundations of Faith-Based Love

The book begins by establishing the fundamental principles of biblical dating. It emphasizes the importance of faith, purpose, and commitment in building a lasting and profound relationship rooted in spirituality.

Chapter 2: Preparing for the Journey Ahead

In Chapter 2, readers learn how to prepare for the journey of finding a soulmate. It discusses self-awareness, the significance of prayer, and the role of friends and mentors in the process.

Chapter 3: The Art of Attraction: Finding Your Potential Soulmate

The third chapter explores the initial stages of attraction, offering insights into how to recognize potential soulmates and navigate the early stages of dating.

Chapter 4: Building a Strong Foundation: The Process of Getting to Know Your Potential Soulmate

Chapter 4 delves into the process of getting to know a potential partner on a deeper level, focusing on emotional intimacy, compatibility assessment, and effective conflict resolution.

Chapter 5: The Road to Commitment: Nurturing a Lasting Partnership

Chapter 5 emphasizes the significance of commitment in a faith-based relationship, offering guidance on deepening the spiritual connection and preparing for marriage.

Chapter 6: The Culmination of Love: Discernment and the Realization of Your Soul's Mate

Chapter 6 is about discerning God's will and recognizing your soul's mate. It covers the role of prayer, seeking counsel, and making informed decisions about the future.

Chapter 7: Nurturing a Lifelong Love: Building a Strong and Lasting

Marriage

In Chapter 7, readers learn how to build and sustain a strong, faith-based marriage. It discusses the importance of maintaining a Christ-centered marriage, effective communication, and the involvement of family and community.

Chapter 8: Thriving Together: Maintaining a Strong, Faith-Based Marriage

Chapter 8 focuses on maintaining a strong faith-based marriage, including strategies for effective communication, conflict resolution, and family life.

Chapter 9: Sharing Your Love Story with the World: Inspiring Others through Faith-Based Love

This chapter discusses the impact of your love story on the world and how to inspire others through your faith-based love. It emphasizes mentoring, community engagement, and leaving a legacy.

Chapter 10: Reflecting on Your Journey: The Impact of Your Love Story

Chapter 10 is a reflection on the impact of your faith-based love story. It underscores the significance of faith, celebrating milestones, and sharing wisdom with others.

Chapter 11: A Journey Without End: The Ever-Evolving Love Story

The penultimate chapter discusses the ongoing nature of your love story and the importance of embracing the unknown. It highlights the growth, continued celebrations, and the legacy of your love story.

Chapter 12: Embracing the Unknown: The Legacy of Faith-Based Love

The final chapter underscores the legacy of faith-based love and the beauty of embracing the unknown. It discusses ongoing mentorship and community engagement, leaving a legacy of faith, and the ever-evolving journey.

"Biblical Dating: Finding Your Soul's Mate" is a comprehensive guide for individuals seeking to find love and build lasting, faith-based relationships.

It is not only a practical manual for navigating the complexities of dating and marriage but also a testament to the enduring power of faith in shaping profound and lasting love stories. Readers are encouraged to embrace the journey and continue to inspire others through their faith-based love.

www.ingramcontent.com/pod-product-compliance
Lightning Source LLC
LaVergne TN
LVHW012132070526
838202LV00056B/5958